The

PROPHETIC STREAM

WILLIAM TABER
Pendle Hill Pamphlet 256

About the Author/ William Taber's roots and life-long membership are among the Conservative (unprogrammed) Friends of Eastern Ohio, but he has also been nurtured by two other styles of Quakerism. As a youth and young man he was active in the Pittsburgh (Friends General Conference) Meeting; and after graduating from Olney Friends School at Barnesville, Ohio, he received a B.A. from William Penn College and an M.A. from Earlham School of Religion, thus becoming acquainted with pastoral Friends (Friends United Meeting) in Iowa and Indiana. He was also a T. Wistar Brown Fellow at Haverford College in 1965-1966, doing research and writing on the history of Conservative Friends.

He taught at Moses Brown School and spent twenty years as teacher or administrator at Olney Friends School. For six years he served Ohio Yearly Meeting as a "Released Friend," which allowed him to reach out to wider Quakerism and ecumenical projects as well as to his own yearly meeting. In 1966 he was recorded as a minister by his meeting at Barnesville, Ohio, which follows the traditional Quaker practice of recording individuals who have a "gift" of ministry in their unprogrammed meetings.

William Taber is entering his fourth year as a teacher at Pendle Hill where he specializes in Quaker Studies and the Prophets, with an interest in prayer, spiritual healing, and in psychic phenomena as related to valid spiritual experience. He is the author of *Be Gentle, Be Plain, A History of Olney* and several articles on Conservative Friends or the Quietist tradition, and he is an occasional speaker or retreat leader on various aspects of Quakerism, prayer, and the spiritual journey.

This pamphlet is an expression of his concern to revive the prophetic element in Quaker worship and ministry as well as in the wider Christian community.

Request for permission to quote or to translate should be addressed to Pendle Hill Publications, Wallingford, Pennsylvania 19086.

Copyright © 1984 by Pendle Hill
ISBN 0-87574-256-4

Library of Congress catalog card number 84-61291

Printed in the United States of America by Sowers Printing Company, Lebanon, Pennsylvania

August, 1984: 6000

"The term *prophetic* indicates in a single word the basic theory of Quaker ministry . . . . a ministry which waits until it becomes a vocal expression of the Divine Word spoken immediately in the heart." When Howard Brinton wrote this in *Prophetic Ministry,* Pendle Hill Pamphlet 54, 1950 (pp.3, 5), he started me on a path of exploration and reflection which has led to this pamphlet.

The Prophets and the Quaker Connection is the title of courses taught at Pendle Hill and Willistown Meeting, and of a series of five talks given at New England Yearly Meeting. This pamphlet is an edited version of the 1983 New England Yearly Meeting talks, which explored the connection between Old and New Testament prophets, Jesus, and Quaker religious experience. Since the focus is on connections, the text moves back and forth across time, and is not intended to be a systematic or scholarly survey either of the prophets or of Quakerism.

My frequent references to George Fox and Quakerism are not intended to imply that there are not many other great souls in other traditions who have also experienced Divine reality in a prophetic and transforming way. These references are intended to show how Fox and the early Quaker experience of "primitive Christianity revived" were related to the experience of earlier prophets and to help modern Friends who often shy away from conventional Christian terminology to understand what Fox may have felt and meant when he used such terms.

MOSES AND THE ROCK WHERE JOY BEGINS

> I want you to know, brethren, that our fathers were all under the cloud, and all passed through the sea, and all were baptized into Moses in the cloud and in the sea, and all ate the same supernatural food and all drank the same supernatural drink. For they drank from the supernatural Rock which followed them, and the Rock was Christ.
>
> I Corinthians 10:1-4

All of the early Friends ministers, starting with George Fox, believed that they were in the living stream of the prophets which stretched from Abraham and Moses through Jesus and the apostles unto their very own time. Those early Quakers acted out their connection with the older prophets, sometimes in very dramatic ways.[1] We modern Friends can deepen our understanding of the Quaker faith by going back to the prophets, reading and "talking" with the prophets in a conversation between the Old Testament prophets, Jesus, George Fox, and ourselves.

This reading of the Old Testament can be difficult for the modern sensitive mind, for the Old Testament world can seem like a wasteland of violent and judgmental language at the behest of an arbitrary God. But if we can read the prophets with George Fox on one shoulder and Jesus on the other, we quickly begin to discover that the seeds of the New Testament are already growing in the Old Testament. Not only in the prophets, but also in other parts of the Old Testament we can see an evolutionary movement toward the radical shift of consciousness that continues into the New Covenant. Looking at the old writings with the eyes of George Fox, as well as with

4

the help of modern scholars, we can find traces and hints of the preexistent Christ, the spirit of the eternal Christ present in the Old Testament pages. In this spirit we can imagine George Fox saying "and the rock which followed Moses was Christ," and we can hear other commentators make a connection between the eternal Christ and the beautiful Old Testament descriptions of the wisdom of God.[2] If we read the Old Testament in this spirit, as George Fox read it, our reading becomes a journey into the gentleness of Christ.

Before we can discuss that "rock which followed Moses," we need to go back to the early part of Moses' story where he seemed to be a complete failure. According to some accounts, he was as old as forty when he had to confront his failure as an upper-class, educated "radical activist" in one of the great civilizations of his time. He had to flee for his life because his passion to help his people had led him to commit a murder for which some of his own people were about to betray him. Then this princely but stuttering man escaped through the Pharoah's border police at the eastern boundaries and on into what the Bible calls Midian, probably in the Sinai Peninsula. His passion for justice was still with him when he came upon a well where he defended and helped the seven daughters of the priest of Midian against a group of burly shepherds. Out of this adventure he gained not only a job, but a wife, for he was taken into the family of Jethro, the priest of Midian.

According to some accounts he spent the next forty years as a faithful son-in-law, husband and shepherd. During this time, he was learning about his religious roots just as many educated people today must pause in the middle of their careers to spend a term at Pendle Hill, Earlham School of Religion, or Woodbrooke in order to reach a deeper level of themselves. Those Sinai years were also like a Pendle Hill experience in that they gave him plenty of space and time to change the busy rhythms of civilization into a more quiet and receptive pace. As was true with George Fox, a part of his training was the solitude of a shepherd.

It was Moses the solitary shepherd, Moses the educated man who had turned to a deeper level of education, who was at last able to see the burning bush, who was able to take off his shoes and step through that flaming doorway into another reality, a level of consciousness which would lead to a new phase of human evolution. The direction of that evolution is suggested by a key passage which, on the surface, is about Moses' asking the proper name for God:

> Then Moses said to God, "If I come to the people of Israel and say to them, 'The God of your fathers has sent me to you,' and they ask me, 'What is his name?' what shall I say to them?" God said to Moses, *"I am who I am."* And he said, "Say this to the people of Israel, *'I am* has sent me to you.' " (Exodus 3:13,14)

Those who can go back to the original meaning of the language say that *I am* could just as easily be translated as *I am being* or *I am existing* or *I am becoming.* Much has been written and preached about this passage; I agree with Martin Buber about its most important meaning.[3] God is livingly present everywhere and everywhen, even in the once proud and now humbled Moses, who could never again be tempted to make the mistake of thinking that God could be localized in a carved chunk of wood or a chiseled slab of stone. It is terrifying, transforming, and mind-shaking to experience the living presence of the living God. We remember how the apostle Paul was knocked to the ground and blinded by that power, and how that experience so shook the early Friends that their spiritual descendents are still called Quakers!

Our reading of the Moses story needs to rest long and lovingly and meditatively upon the *I am* passage, for it calls forth the early Quaker experience of a human-divine relationship so intense and so pervasive that it can only be described as a shift in the level of consciousness. For George Fox, "all creation had a new smell." According to the New Testament, we are transformed in "the mind of Christ" (I Corinthians 2).

If the gospel of John is right, the preexistent Christ, the Word, the feminine Wisdom of God was present with and in Moses as he stood barefoot at the flaming bush. As Moses turned away from that place, he carried with him not a creed nor a set of magic words but an expanded consciousness which would always be in touch with God; he was not so much a theologian who could say the right words as a man of faith who was in touch with reality. However we describe that encounter with God and however we describe that faith, Moses had become a man of vision, of power, of courage and, says the Bible, of great meekness. The formerly ineffective "social activist" now proceeds to change history, becoming the foundation and the archetype of all the Biblical prophets who followed him.

From the stories of Moses and the prophets who followed him, we learn of three major tasks of a prophet. Put very simply, the prophet's first task is to discover the law; the second task is to show how the law can—or must—be put into practice; and the third task is to make spirit available. At first glance these three tasks seem to ignore the commonly understood idea of the prophet as one who predicts the future, especially a future of doom. However, as we look at the biblical use of the word *prophet,* as well as at the Quaker experience of prophecy, the commonly understood idea expands in meaning.

The first task of the prophet is to discover, or to recover, or to reinterpret law. In the book of First Samuel the old word for prophet was *seer,* suggesting that the prophet is a person who can see beneath and beyond the surface of things. As we look at the words of prophet after prophet, we gradually realize that their warnings, their advice, their visions of the future are usually based upon a solid understanding or *seeing* of the law.

Perhaps you, like me, have had trouble with the ancient laws handed down by Moses. I accepted the Ten-Commandment-core with a Sunday School deference which could never quite make the laws of Moses as real or as important as the laws of science. For me, this unreality of the key Old Testament laws began to change when I began to read the Bible in what I sometimes call the Quaker way—that is, reading with both the analytical mind and the intuitive mind leaving plenty of space for the Holy Spirit to operate, to integrate.[4] On the one hand such reading makes use of Biblical scholarship and all the light that modern science can provide; on the other hand, using this method, one reads softly, and deeply, and meditatively, with the intellect temporarily at rest. One simply savors and rests in the meaning instead of analyzing it; one just pauses from time to time to stare off into space and wait for what earlier Friends called "the inward motion."

As I reread the Old Testament laws in this more meditative way, two recognitions helped open my understanding of the reality of these laws for us today. First, I realized, as did George Fox, that most of the laws of Moses found in Exodus, Leviticus, Numbers, and Deuteronomy were designed for a specific culture of long ago. Many Bible scholars can even show us how they believe the laws evolved during the centuries before the first five books of the Old Testament took their final form.[5] Then I began to face the cultural trappings or rubbish with which I had surrounded the concept of law; I realized that I had connected law with fallible legislators, with judges and policemen and with childhood memories of the many adults who ruled my life with a myriad of laws.

Given these recognitions, there is still a small living core of the Law of Moses which remains as vital as it ever was. In order to go back to that living core of Moses' Law I had to go back to that quiet, calm inward place so dear to the Quaker where I could begin to imagine what it must have been like for Newton slowly and then exultantly to intuit some of the laws which hold the universe—and even these our bodies—together. Experiencing this sense of discovery brings us back closer to the early word for prophet as the seer, the one who sees deep into the nature of things and sees patterns of order which the rest of us cannot yet see. Thus, Moses, like all true prophets, was truly a seer, for like Newton and Einstein he saw or felt the law as a vital force, not merely as a string of words. I have little doubt that he actually heard the words of the Ten Commandments on Sinai. I also believe that he could not have done what he did if he had not also *seen* how these laws were an indispensible part of the fabric of the new age fellowship he was to build.

I often find it useful to go back to the Ten Commandments and to contemplate, in the seer-like fashion I have just described, what they can mean to us still. In fact, they can be used as a set of queries for personal examination. In contrast to most of the other laws which were clearly meant for a patriarchal and rather violent era, the distilled wisdom of the Ten Commandments applies even across thirty-five centuries. This is especially true of the first four commandments as a unit, which we might describe as the focus commandments, or a set of principles on how to focus our vital energies or life force.

> And God spoke all these words, saying, ''I am the Lord your God, who brought you out of the land of Egypt, out of the house of bondage. You shall have no other Gods before me.'' (Exodus 20:1,2)

Our Western and ambitious minds readily accept the concept that without discrimination, without focus, our energies are dissipated and we achieve little. If we can forget for a moment the emotional objection many of us have to the concept of a "jealous God" (our modern sensibilities may read this as an egocentric, touchy, insecure God), we can see, in that quiet inward state, that the first commandment is nothing else than a powerful call to be powerfully focused around one supreme loyalty, one absolute and unshakable trust. An experienced "friend of God" knows that such a clear focus, such a trust and loyalty cannot come from the intellect alone, nor can such a "friend of God" depend merely on emotions for such a profound and unswayable focus; rather (at least in the Quaker tradition), such a person sinks into that quiet place within to see and know and taste and touch that this commandment is a rock on which to build, is a focus, is a connection into Life itself. With our modern understanding of ecological interdependence, with increasing awareness that we are in some mysterious way at one with the Moslem, the Jew, the Hindu and the Marxist through the life force which forms our tiny planet, the contemplation of this first focus commandment does not divide us, but draws us into a place of centeredness from which it is possible to begin to find the energy and the good will to work tirelessly on behalf of the new age. In other words, this first query of Moses simply and quietly asks the question, "Where is your loyalty; where is your rock-solid, unshakable trust? Is that trust single and unshakable, or do you really act as if there were many 'gods' and therefore scatter and diffuse your energies?" Or to paraphrase Jesus, the second Moses, "Has the salt lost its savor so that it is therefore unfocused, useless?"

The second focus commandment simply expands on the first one:

"You shall not make for yourself a graven image, or any likeness of anything that is in heaven above, or that is in the earth beneath, or that is in the water under the earth; you shall not bow down to them or serve them." (Exodus 20:4,5)

Then there follows another use of that difficult term for us—*a jealous God.* As we read and ponder that commandment in the inward quiet place, and as our reading is informed by the spirit and words of Jesus, we realize that ascribing jealousy to God is an earlier, more primitive way of understanding the inexorable laws of focus. If we translate this commandment into a Quaker advice and query, we realize that we are being warned of the endless temptation to scatter our forces by focusing on one or more other aspects of reality than that one supreme loyalty established in the first commandment. In that quiet inward place, we can hear the gentle query, "What are your graven images? To what do you give the loyalty due only to God? Is it career? Is it a passion to be accepted by others? Or is it some fear?" Although by *graven image* Moses clearly meant a physical representation in stone or clay or wood or metal, the modern mind can see that creeds, philosophies, the best of social change movements, even religions *can* become, in effect, graven images which deflect and scatter our forces.

"You shall not take the name of the Lord your God in vain; for the Lord will not hold him guiltless who takes his name in vain" (Exodus 20:7). The third commandment goes far beyond the banning of profanity, for it is also a reminder of the powerful laws of focus. One might even call it an early forerunner of the science of semantics, which tells us that the word is not the same as the thing it represents. I often think that

11

"profanity is prayer gone wrong," that much of the profanity we hear can be traced back to a time when these words were uttered as brief prayers for Divine help; but gradually these prayers became automatic and degenerated into ejaculative sounds. Other forms of profanity which call for damnation of another represent, according to Jesus, a vicious and dangerous perversion of the Life Force. This simple commandment reminds us, then, of the power of really living in *this* moment, of being present where we are and of really understanding and meaning what we say. The commandment cautions us that rightly to utter the Name of God is to bring the whole focus of our being into the vortex of that center of energy and awesome power. To utter that Name, to open the conduit of that megavoltage power lightly or with only a lazy fraction of our attention is to court disaster for the spiritually developed soul. To speak frivolously simply numbs us to the beauty and the anguish and the divine tasks of the Eternal Now. It is no accident that our Quaker forbearers were sometimes ridiculed for their passion to use only the exactly correct word, even in ordinary, casual conversation. They took no words, of any kind, in vain. Because they kept the powerful focus even in little things, they kept the faith.

The fourth focus commandment to "remember the sabbath day, to keep it holy" may seem out of date for those of us who remember the old blue laws and the strong Protestant concern to keep the Sabbath as a special and, some would say, a rather dull day. Yet Moses, of all people, was against dull days; his dull days ended forever when he had experienced the awesome power of the Living Presence. This focus commandment is a reminder of the absolute importance of periodically stopping our outward activity to give the intuitive mode of our being a chance to operate. The Sabbath is a day or a time for relationship and family and community, instead of sharp individualism; it is a time for feeling, for appreciating, for sensing rather than competing and judging and grasping. And yes, it can be a time for becoming aware of pain and disharmony. It is usually in this Sabbath place, this intuitive mode, that the prophet begins to suffer the anguish and disharmony of the world and where the prophet begins to see the vision of how to mend it. What else is a "silent" Friends meeting for worship but the focus of this focus? It is wonderful if this calm, receptive focus can be extended throughout one whole day, or at least during daily silent times; and it would be wonderful if more of us were in that state George Fox spoke of, of being beyond the flaming sword, of being, like Moses, in constant touch with the Divine.[6] But since we are not, we probably need this commandment's reminder that a truly focused life must have periodic times of the Sabbath state of consciousness.

When Moses came back down the mountain with the Ten Commandments (and the more parochial and time-bound elements of the law which are not so relevant to us today), he began to perform the second task of the prophet—to inspire, to lead, to organize, to legislate a way of life, to develop a life style in accord with the law; to help generate an ethic, a culture, a civilization in harmony with the law at the center of all life. Another way to describe this second task of the prophet is to say that the prophet must walk in the new law and show others how to walk in it.

And so Moses called the Children of Israel together to join them to each other and to God in a covenant, a very important step in the development of human consciousness. George Fox and other religious leaders have rightly called this the Old Covenant, a covenant which was to be superceded when a new prophet like Moses would come with a New Covenant written in the human heart. On a simple literal level, the word *covenant* simply means agreement, more formal than, but similar to, the term used by Jesus when he said, "Again I say to you, if two of you agree on earth about anything they ask, it will be done for them by my Father in heaven" (Mt. 18:19). Moses' covenant and Jesus' use of the word *agree* go far beyond a simple concurrence; the Old Covenant of Moses and the New Covenant of Jesus imply a deep connectedness with life itself; they imply a focus so profound that both our inward trust in God and our outward steadfastness are unshakable.

The Old Covenant of Moses was sealed and empowered in a way that the modern mind often finds difficult. At a place and time in history in which animal sacrifice was almost universal, Moses sacrificed bulls, and the blood was saved in great basins. Apparently the people of that time and place believed that the essential and indissoluble life force of an animal was contained in its blood. Moses took half of this blood and dashed it upon the high altar, representing God, and then he turned and threw the other half over the people. If we understand their belief about the unity of the blood of an animal, then we see that Moses had joined the people to each other and to God with a holy glue, an indissoluble bond. Pondering this practice has helped me to understand a little better what our evangelical Friends mean when they speak of the Blood of Christ of the New Covenant.

George Fox also helped me when he wrote this passage in his *Journal:*

As they were discoursing of it, I saw, through the immediate opening of the invisible Spirit, the blood of Christ. And I cried out among them, and said, "Do ye not see the blood of Christ? See it in your hearts, to sprinkle your hearts and consciences from dead works to serve the living God?" For I saw it, the blood of the New Covenant, how it came into the heart. This startled the professors, who would have the blood only without [outside of] them and not in them.[7]

14

I commend this early passage in Fox's journal because of the spiritual and ethical content he gives to that usually very doctrinal expression, *blood of Christ*. In this, as in so many other ways, George Fox was both an orthodox Christian and a very unorthodox one because he went beyond the surface of the literal doctrinal words to discover the living essense of the New Covenant, to experience that vast connectedness between humanity and God, to discover the indissoluble bond, that holy glue, that Life and Light and Power which burst in upon Moses as he stood beside the burning bush. Thus, by leading his people into covenant and by continuing to lead them during forty dry years, Moses demonstrated the second function of the prophet, showing the way to live the law, showing how to walk with God into a better future.

In showing the way to live the Law or to walk with God, Moses also performed the third task of the prophet by helping make spirit available, particularly through prayer and intercession. At first, this function may not seem to fit the conventional picture of the prophet. However, if we go back to some of the early recognition of prophets in the book of Genesis, we discover that the prophet was thought of as a person who was very close to God and who had the power effectively to pray for other people. Moses himself is a good example of a great prophet who was moved to pray and intercede for the people. This tradition of the prophet as interceder becomes very strong when we get to the prophet Jeremiah; some of the ancient commentaries and traditions about him put great stress on his almost sacrificial prayers for the people, and we get further hints of this prophetic tradition in the beautiful, enigmatic servant passages in what is today called Second Isaiah. The early Christians saw Jesus as perfectly fulfilling this prophetic role of interceding on behalf of others and making the Holy Spirit available. On one level the prayer of the Old Testament prophet could be seen as bringing merely material blessings to those who were prayed for, but we must remember that the Old Testament writers believed that material blessings resulted from spiritual and moral harmony, or righteousness, so that even on this level, the prophet had to make spirit available for material results. In this light, we can look upon the blood which Moses used to seal the Old Covenant not merely as physical blood, but as a sign, symbol and seal of the living spiritual bond which would unite his people with God for many centuries. In other words, by using the physical metaphor or symbol available in his time, he, like other prophets, made spirit available to the people.

Many troubles plagued Moses and his new, covenanted people during their long years of wandering. Even when the people lost their faith, Moses was sustained by the Living Presence which had discovered and transformed him. George Fox quoted and paraphrased a strange expression from First Corinthians, ''and the rock which followed them was Christ'' (see I Corinthians 10:4).[8] Apparently Paul knew the rabbinic tradition that God had caused a supernatural rock to follow Moses during the years of wandering, so that whenever there was great need for water, Moses could strike the rock as he is recorded to have done on two occasions, and the water would flow miraculously to the people. Paul, with his belief in the preexistent Christ, believed that the ever-present rock and the supernatural, life-giving water was actually the preexistent or eternal Christ, and George Fox echoed that belief, adding new dimensions to our understanding of Moses as the archetype and foundation of all the prophets. George Fox evidently believed that the universal and eternal Light of Christ was present as a living stream in the midst of the transformation of Moses at the burning bush, and that it was present like a seed in all of the law revealed through Moses, and that it was present throughout Moses' life as nourishing, spiritual water.

George Fox would probably say that the rock which followed Moses still follows us today. He might remind us that if we do not see that living, present rock, or if we do not always feel nourished by its spiritual waters, it may be because we have forgotten the timeless focus of the four Focus Commandments of the Law of Moses.

IS CATCHING PROPHECY LIKE CATCHING THE MEASLES?

Is catching prophecy like catching the measles? Is it a divine contagion which can be caught from an infected group of people? Or is a prophetic career something one can prepare for in a school for the prophets? Or does prophecy occur only at the command of God? The Old Testament prophets, the New Testament prophets, and even the Quaker prophets all tell us that true prophecy is always the gift of God, and that it comes only at the divine initiative. Even so, many of the prophets act as if the willingness and the ability to be a prophet can at least be caught, and perhaps even taught, so long as we remember that the fact of prophecy remains with God alone. This theory of divine contagion grows out of the third task of the prophet, which is to make spirit available.

An early example of catching prophecy, or of a prophet helping to make spirit available, occurs in the eleventh chapter of Numbers, where Moses and the seventy elders conduct what might be called (if we take some liberties in interpretation) ''the first Quaker meeting in the Bible.'' Not long after the great tent of the tabernacle and all of its fittings had been completed at Sinai, and the many years of wandering had begun, Moses and his people encamped at a dry and barren place called Kib'roth-hatta'avah', where the people bitterly complained, so that what the Bible calls the "fire of the Lord" burned among them, and Moses prayed, stopping the destruction. But still the people complained and yearned for the meats and foods of Egypt until Moses had had just about all he could take of the burden of his lonely leadership. Finally, God told him:

> "Gather for me seventy men of the elders of Israel, whom you know to be elders of the people and officers over them; and bring them to the tent of meeting, and let them take their stand there with you. And I will come down and talk with you there; and I will take some of the spirit which is upon you and put it upon them; and they shall bear the burden of the people with you, that you may not bear it yourself alone." (Numbers 11:16, 17)

And so it came about that Moses gathered seventy elders at the tabernacle, and the spirit of the Lord came down to Moses and put some of the spirit, which Moses had formerly borne alone, into the seventy elders; "and when the spirit rested upon them, they prophesied" (Numbers 11:25).

No one can say for sure exactly what the old account meant by the word *prophesied;* I assume that the elders were in some degree of altered state of consciousness. They might have been speaking ecstatically at the same time, as in a modern Pentecostal service, or singing or dancing, or speaking as seers one at a time, or they could even have been silently quaking as they experienced the new dimension of being open to the Holy Spirit. Sadly, the account suggests that the elders did not again have such a gathered meeting.

But there were "Quaker mavericks" even then. Eldad and Medad, two men who were apparently elders but who were not for some reason at the meeting of the seventy elders, began to prophesy in the camp, creating a sense of scandal among those who believed that holy things can happen only in holy places; and Moses' minister, Joshua, cried out, "My lord Moses, forbid them!" George Fox must have loved this early biblical evidence that true worship and prophecy can occur outside of a church. In defense of the Quaker practice of prophetic ministry, Fox sometimes quoted Moses' answer to Joshua: "Are you jealous for my sake? Would that all the Lord's people were prophets, that the Lord would put his spirit upon them!" (Numbers 11:28, 29)

The coming of the Spirit to the seventy elders did not occur in a vacuum, for as elders they would have had experience and some training, perhaps by Moses himself. They certainly went through rituals of preparation before being open to the power of God. They were together in a group in a holy place, and they were in the presence of a prophet of great power. All of these circumstances would have made it easier for these prepared people to receive the Spirit of God when it poured out upon them. In other words, they were in ideal circumstances to "catch" prophecy. But what about the two mavericks, Eldad and Medad? Their story tells us that the power of God is always reaching outside of the religious establishment, beyond the facing bench and the inner council of ministers and elders. Even this early in the Old Testament we have the example of the prophets Eldad and Medad operating as a pair, just as Jesus sent his seventy out two by two, and just as, in at least some parts of the early Christian Church, the prophets travelled in pairs, and as it was once the common pattern for travelling Quaker ministers to have at least one companion.

About two centuries later the story of the boy Samuel is another good example of catching prophecy. His mother dedicated Samuel while he was still a child to live in the sacred shrine where the Ark of Moses was still kept (See I Samuel, ch. 1-3). Thus he lived continually in the presence of the holy.

19

As he watched the rituals and listened to the chants and prayers, the Spirit must have etched the power of God deeply into his subconscious just as the same Spirit would have affected a Quaker child of several generations ago who listened to the daily family Bible reading and who settled into several deep silences with family or school every day. The boy Samuel, like future Quaker prophets, was deeply schooled, even before he was ready to read, in the rhythms and patterns and language which led to God. In time the boy was trusted to remain alone in the sanctuary before the sacred ark, or perhaps an altar, being present before the Lord long into the night. Finally, God spoke to this prepared youth while he slept or drowsed in that sacred place. Samuel caught prophecy even though he was not seeking to be a prophet; he was surprised by the voice of God and did not even recognize it at first. He is a good example of how a solitary individual, who has become practiced in the rhythms and rituals of faith, and who relaxes so that the aperture of the intuitive mind is consciously or unconsciously open to the divine, can "catch" prophecy at an unexpected time. Samuel was also fortunate that he had a teacher in old blind Eli, who finally realized what was happening to Samuel and who gave him some instruction about living in the prophetic stream. Would that our Society of Friends and other churches had more teachers to help our tender new prophets as they tremble or teeter at that new place.

I know of one beautiful modern example of a living Friend who came to this new place in a solitary way. This lifelong Quaker, a skilled craftsman, was well past middle age when he felt nudged to begin daily devotional reading and worship in the early morning before he went to work. He had done this for many months with no significant change when, as he put it, he sat down one morning and looked into his heart, and he knew "that Someone had been there" because of the new life

20

and genuine gentleness which he suddenly and unexpectedly found there. I like that story because, for this man there was no need for the laying on of hands to bring the Holy Spirit, nor did this man even need to be in a gathered meeting of Quaker prophets to "catch" the spirit. In time he became empowered with a gift of gentle, discerning, and prophetic ministry. In a way he had prepared for this by a lifetime of living out the Quaker rhythms; in a way he prepared for this by doing the early morning reading and worship; but only when God was ready did my friend unexpectedly "catch" the spirit, the way one might catch the measles, without warning.

When Samuel had become old, and Israel was in need of a new and different leader, we see one more example of how the spirit of prophecy might be caught. Saul, a younger man in search of his father's strayed livestock, came to Samuel the seer for advice in this very practical matter, as was the custom in those days. According to the story in the ninth and tenth chapters of I Samuel, the seer-prophet Samuel already knew through the Holy Spirit that a very special person was approaching, and Samuel had the discernment instantly to recognize Saul as that person when he saw him at the gate of the city. And so the great prophet took the stranger up to a sacred high place, probably a temple or sanctuary above the city, where a group of selected people took part in a ritual sacrifice and the sacred feast which followed it. In our terms, it was a kind of communion service and love feast with political overtones. To his surprise, Saul was given a place of honor and was served the largest and most honorable piece of meat, which having come from a sacrificial animal and thus being shared with God, was both communion with God and a fellowship feast. Before Samuel sent Saul and his servant on their way the next morning, he performed the prophetic act of preparing another person to enter the prophetic stream. They stopped pri-

21

vately (the servant had already been sent ahead) and Samuel told the astonished and perhaps shy, younger man of his destiny. Then he anointed and kissed him, and gave him specific directions:

> "You will meet a band of prophets coming down from the high place with harp, tambourine, flute and lyre before them, prophesying. Then the spirit of the Lord will come mightily upon you and you shall prophesy with them and be turned into another man." (I Samuel 10:5,6)

Later in that same day, Saul did meet the band of prophets and from them he did catch prophecy, and he did become, as Samuel had predicted, another man.[1] Though catching prophecy is not quite so simple as catching the measles, there is some truth in the idea. Even the fragmentary and sometimes puzzling Old Testament record makes it clear that people are more likely to catch prophecy from contact with other prophets, especially when one prophet can prepare and instruct a person who is susceptible to the prophetic infection. Sometimes this prophetic infection is an ecstatic experience, as it often appeared to be in the descriptions of the bands of prophets, or it can be a great trouble and a true dis-ease, as it was for the prophet Jeremiah, who described it as "a burning fire shut up in my bones, and I am weary with holding it in, and I cannot" (Jeremiah 20:9). Sometimes the discernment about a prophet-to-be and the initial preparation begins many years in advance, as when Rufus Jones' Aunt Peace prophesied over him as an infant, or when a visiting minister laid his hand on the boy Gilbert Thomas in a meeting house yard in rural Ohio, or when the infant Jesus received the blessing of Simeon and Anna.

As the rest of the Old Testament story unfolds after the time of Samuel, we get tantalizing glimpses, here and there, of groups of prophets, sometimes called bands, or in later times, "Sons of the Prophets" who practiced a kind of group worship in which consciousness was altered and opened to ecstatic or prophetic states. It is even possible, though there is no clear evidence for this, that there were links between these groups and at least some of the great prophets who gave their names to the prophetic books at the end of the Old Testament. There is more evidence that some of the great prophets had disciples who stayed together after the prophet's death, preserving the tradition, and perhaps providing a nurturing ground for new prophets.[2]

The prophetic opening of Jesus had been prepared by other prophets from his infancy and even before his birth. There is a wealth of unproved speculation, and some non-Biblical tradition, that he was in touch, during the hidden years of his young manhood, with local or distant groups who gave him further preparation for his great prophetic task. When the fullness of the Spirit came to Jesus, he was in the presence of other prophetic persons, his cousin John and John's disciples. Thus, in a way, Jesus' experience paralleled that of many preceding lesser prophets who had caught prophecy in the presence of another prophet or group of prophets.

Like Moses, Jesus proclaimed a new law growing out of the old; like Moses he performed miracles, especially miracles of healing, miracles in which he made spirit available to affect first the spiritual, and then the physical plane. Then, like other prophets before and since, he was martyred, but the power which flowed from his self-giving makes him unique among prophets. Fifty days after his martyrdom, a power which would change the face of all subsequent history invaded and possessed the tiny band of disciples and followers which he, like earlier prophets, had left behind him. Whereas Moses had to face this awesome energy, this breathtaking expansion of consciousness and its terrible responsibility alone, the disciples on the day of Pentecost may have numbered 120 people when they received, or caught, the Holy Spirit which Jesus the martyred prophet and more than prophet had released when he, as the end and the fulfillment of the prophets, made spirit available in a new way to the whole world.

From the early Quaker point of view the Book of Acts is really the story of how that Spirit became more and more available in the ancient world. When the apostles in Jerusalem learned that the new Christians in Samaria had not yet received the Holy Spirit *even though they had been baptized in water,* they sent the weighty apostles Peter and John to them, so that they might enter into the spiritual baptism and new life of the Holy Spirit, or to use our metaphor once again, Peter and John went to the Samaritans to help them ''catch'' the spirit, the spirit from which prophecy comes (Acts 8:14-17). Another episode which must have interested the early Friends occurred when the Holy Spirit fell on the Roman centurian Cornelius and his household even before they had said the proper doctrinal words and *before they had been outwardly baptised with water.* Here again, we see the phenomenon of ''catching'' the spirit in the presence of a prophet who was full of it. Peter had just seen a vision which opened the way for him to reach out to gentiles when messengers from Cornelius arrived to ask Peter to come and explain the new faith. Thus, Peter and his companions, when they finally arrived at the home of Cornelius, found a prepared household almost ready to receive and believe. So Peter preached to them with such power that:

> While Peter was still saying this, the Holy Spirit fell on all who heard the word. And the believers from among the circumcised who came with Peter were amazed, because the gift of the Holy Spirit had been poured out even on the Gentiles. . . . . Then Peter declared, ''Can anyone forbid water for baptizing these people who have received the Holy Spirit just as we have?'' (Acts 10:44-47)

It is clear from these stories and the fact that the term *Holy Spirit* occurs about seventeen more times in the book of Acts that each Christian was expected to have "caught" the Holy Spirit, usually from someone else who had it. Acts also makes it clear that being in the Holy Spirit was an experience which other Christians could recognize; it was not just a metaphor or a theological term. The book of Acts shows that many important decisions were the result of direct guidance by the Holy Spirit; sometimes this guidance was spoken through Christians recognized as prophets. Acts mentions such prophets four distinct times, suggesting that they played an important role in the life of the early church (See Acts 11:27; 13:1-3; 15:28,32; 16:6; 21:10,11).

In the twelfth and fourteenth chapters of I Corinthians, Paul makes it sound as if prophecy were very common. In fact, his advice in the fourteenth chapter suggests that nearly everyone in the church of Corinth wanted to prophesy. We might say that he was asking them to slow down their "popcorn meeting," for he said, "Let two or three prophets speak, and let the others weigh what is said. If a revelation is made to another sitting by, let the first be silent" (I Corinthinans 14:29,30). George Fox believed that because the Corinthians obviously needed so much advice and direction to keep their worship services from getting out of hand, they had not yet come into the full maturity of the Holy Spirit; they had not yet passed beyond the flaming sword back into that full communion with God which Adam and Eve had known in the Garden of Eden. Therefore, said Fox, it was natural for Paul to relegate women to an inferior position in that church (as they had been under the law of Moses) until such time as that church had entered into the full state of perfection in Christ, and they were no longer under the old law. He believed that if they were fully come into the New Covenant and the Holy Spirit, there would be no need for human direction of worship, and men and women would be truly equal in Christ as Fox believed they were and should be in the Society of Friends.[3]

Because the early Friends, unlike the Corinthians, *had* experienced harmony in their meetings, and because they *had* experienced spiritual equality between men and women, they believed that they had entered into the same, living prophetic stream which flowed from far back in the Old Testament and which had been expanded in the New Covenant given by Jesus, the prophet "like unto Moses" who, through the giving of himself in the third task of the prophet, had made spirit richly available to all creation. It is no wonder, then, that early Quaker ministers spoke with the authority and the language of the Old Testament prophets, and it is not surprising that some of them acted out their prophecies in dramatic ways, like the prophets of old.

Just as the Biblical prophets often "caught" their prophecy from another prophet, so it has often been with Quaker ministers, or Quaker prophets across three hundred years. Careful reading of the journals and other accounts shows that in every generation it was the travelling Quaker ministers who were often the most important forces in discerning and encouraging the men and women who were to be raised up as ministers and prophets for the next generation.[4]

On the other hand, there is also evidence that some of our Quaker leaders discovered or "caught" their Quakerism like the measles, not from one person but, like Saul with the band of prophets, they caught it in the power of a gathered meeting. Stephen Grellet, who could hardly understand or speak English, was drawn into that new state of consciousness and received his prophetic commission in a meeting where he was not well-known, and in which he could scarcely understand the spoken ministry in English. Caroline Stephen's often-quoted passage about her first Quaker meeting is another good example.[5]

As Paul says beautifully in Corinthians, when we catch prophecy, or more properly, when we are caught up in the prophetic stream of the Holy Spirit, we do not all become speaking prophets, and that's good, for otherwise our meetings might become as noisy as the Corinthian Church. However, we can all expect to be prophets in the sense of being very close to the Divine and thus we become prophets in sensitivity to the law of the New Age, the New Covenant; therefore we become prophets in the way we live our lives, just as John Woolman altered his clothing, his food, and even the way he travelled because of his prophetic sensitivity. We become prophets in the way we spend our money, in the causes we support, and even where we work and where we live.

We generally think of prophets as dramatic and conspicuous people; not only are they sometimes martyred, they occasionally sit on facing benches, make speeches, get arrested, and are generally in the limelight. We need those conspicuous and bold prophets, and from time to time, even the most unassuming Quaker must take such a stand. However, the Society of Friends would soon die out if we could not depend on the silent and inconspicuous prophets who are necessary for each gathered meeting, for if they do not stay faithfully in that living center, how can others "catch" the spirit which leads us and holds us together? Robert Barclay described this beautifully three centuries ago when he told how the secret, silent, inconspicuous prayer and silent ministry of just one person could lift and center an entire meeting.[6] I know that my own ability to speak or minister in a meeting has often depended on the faithfulness of a few focused, silent prophets. A truly gathered meeting is a band of prophets—silent prophets resting quietly in the prophetic stream so that others who come can catch the spirit in that gathered meeting.

Opening Some Key Words From The Prophets

Four key words or ideas from the great prophets still speak powerfully to us, especially as we see how they were expanded by Jesus and how they became important to the Society of Friends through the prophetic stream of the Holy Spirit, that ageless stream of living and growing experience. These key words so dear to the great Hebrew prophets from the eighth century onward help to counteract a common assumption that the prophets were merely ecstatic, visionary, "doomish," and other-worldly people. A careful reading of their words makes it clear that these prophets were solidly grounded in their mathematical and scientific certainty about the Law by which all life rises or falls. Above all else they knew the Law, like the Psalmist who said, "But his delight is in the law of the Lord, and on this law he meditates day and night" (Psalm 1:2).

The first of these key words is one which we often translate as *justice,* a concept at the heart of all the laws of Moses. When our modern minds look beyond the eye-for-an-eye and other violent aspects of that male-dominated culture of the Old Covenant, we find a strong and continuing demand for justice, especially for the weak, the helpless, the poor, and the stranger. Even if, as some scholars suggest, some of these laws were finally put into writing several centuries after Moses, it is probable that they came from a spoken tradition reaching back to Moses himself.

A dramatic example of the prophets' demand for justice came when the charismatic King David broke at least four of the Ten Commandments by committing adultery with Bathsheba and then arranging for her husband to be killed in battle. Neither David's charm nor his absolute power as an oriental monarch saved him from denunciation by the prophet Nathan, who gives us the tradition that neither kings nor American presidents are above the law (II Samuel, chapters 11 and 12). Thanks to the prophets, we have inherited this ancient tradition that justice must protect each person, especially the weak against the strong. A few generations later the same insistence that the king and the queen are not above the law was proclaimed by that athletic prophet Elijah, as told in the twenty-first chapter of I Kings. On this occasion, King Ahab had coveted a vineyard owned by Naboth, who refused to sell, even to the king. Consequently, Queen Jezebel arranged for witnesses to accuse Naboth falsely, so that he was executed. This execution allowed Ahab to go ahead and appropriate the land he had so much coveted. What Elijah said to Ahab was not very tactful or tasteful by modern standards, but clearly Elijah knew the law of justice for the less powerful and was willing to run great risks in proclaiming it.

About a hundred years after Elijah, a new kind of prophet began to appear, first in the northern kingdom of Israel and soon also in the southern kingdom of Judah. Unlike many of the earlier prophets, these men do not appear to have belonged to bands of ecstatic prophets, even though they often had disciples who preserved their words and put them into writing. Furthermore, these great prophets or "writing prophets," as they are sometimes called, were not interested in being miracle workers or the sort of seer who could find a lost coin, for they had more important work to do. They believed themselves called to be signposts at a traumatic crossroads of history.

The first of these lonely men was Amos of Tekoa, thought by some to be a poor country herdsman and husbandman, though I am inclined to believe that he was a hard working, rustic small landowner and probably a successful trader who had travelled as far north as the rich city of Samaria, the capital of the northern kingdom, or to Bethel, the lavish holy city and shrine of that kingdom. God gave Amos, and the prophets who followed him for about two centuries, a deep and fore-boding sense that something had gone dreadfully wrong with the Holy Experiment of the Covenant of Moses. He knew that a law as real and inexorable as the law of gravity was about to work itself out to a terrible end unless people began to observe the Law. He knew that the class-conscious and hedonistic cul-ture of the northern kingdom was destined to collapse, even though when he first began to proclaim his message the nation was richer and more powerful than ever before.

The key word, or the essence of Amos' message, which reaches across 2800 years of culture and language is the same word we encountered with Elijah: *justice*. Amos' first con-demnation of Israel complains of their selling ''the righteous for silver, and the needy for a pair of shoes—they that trample the head of the poor into the dust of the earth, and turn aside the way of the afflicted'' (Amos 2:6,7). In other words, he mentions the sin of injustice before he mentions improper kinds of worship. Throughout this short book Amos scornfully gives many examples of the great injustice and insensitivity of the ruling classes. Here are just a few of his expressions:

> O you who turn justice to wormwood, and cast down righteousness to the earth! . . . You trample the poor and take from him exactions of wheat, you have built houses of hewn stone. . . . You who afflict the righteous, . . . take a bribe, and turn aside the needy at the gate. (Amos 5:7,11,12)

For Amos, righteousness and justice are inseparable; we can-not have the one without the other. In fact, if there is no righ-teousness, if there is no observing of the inward-outward laws of focus *and* justice, then our religious services, our Bible classes, and our good meetings for worship are of no value, for in the same chapter God (through Amos) condemns empty ritual:

> "I hate, I despise your feasts, and I take no delight in your solemn assemblies. Even though you offer me your burnt offerings and cereal offerings, I will not accept them, and the peace offerings of your fatted beasts I will not look upon. Take away from me the noise of your songs; to the melody of your harps I will not listen." (Amos 5:21-23)

Amos summarizes his whole book for us in the one short verse which follows that strong condemnation of empty ritual: "But let justice roll down like waters, and righteousness like an everflowing stream" (Amos 5:24). We can trace this theme of justice through all the prophets until it expands into broad new meaning in Second Isaiah and in the message and mission of Jesus.

Amos leads us into one of the key ideas of our next prophet, Hosea, when he warns:

> "Behold, the days are coming," says the Lord God, "when I will send a famine on the land; not a famine of bread, nor a thirst for water, but of hearing the words of the Lord. They shall wander from sea to sea, and from north to east; they shall run to and fro to seek the word of the Lord, but they shall not find it." (Amos 8:11,12)

Gentle Hosea actually lived in the northern kingdom, which was totally wiped out just a few years after he had prophesied and pleaded to prevent that famine of the words of the Lord. One of his key words for averting that destruction was *da'ath,* which we sometimes translate as *knowledge.* He cried out for the Lord:

> My people are destroyed for lack of knowledge; because you have rejected knowledge, I reject you from being a priest to me. And since you have forgotten the law of your God, I also will forget your children. (Hosea 4:6)

He proclaims this indictment even at the beginning of the same chapter: "There is no faithfulness or kindness, and no knowledge of God in the land." He then lists, in the following

31

verses, the outward sins and violence which result from such lack of the knowledge of God. Of special interest to the modern reader who is aware of the psychic realm and of the influence of spirit on the surrounding ecology is the third verse:

> Therefore the land mourns, and all who dwell in it languish, and also the beasts of the field, and the birds of the air; and even the fish of the sea are taken away. (Hosea 4:3)

Hosea implies that the *inward* fact of *knowledge* of the Lord, or *knowing* the Lord, is the central inward reality from which flows the *outward* behavior of fulfilling the specific laws of the Covenant. Perhaps you, like me, have been troubled or even irritated by some earnest soul who would look you in the eye and say, "Do you know the Lord?" Even so, it is well for us to ponder this question, for it was important to Hosea as he sought to prevent that terrible national collapse; it was important to Jesus; and it was important to George Fox.

To *know* the Lord is, first of all, to return to the Covenant relationship, just as a citizen of old *knew* his sovereign; that is, the citizen of old *knew* the comfort and security of being under the king's protection, knew the importance of instantly obeying the sovereign's command. That is not too hard to translate for the modern mind, even for one which doesn't view God in a personal way. To recognize the king is another way of allowing the solitary ego and our individualism to fall away in the face of a higher loyalty. The recognition allows us to accept and relax in our smallness, our bondedness with others in the covenant, and in our connection with all life. We know that when we have need the Goodness at the heart of the universe will protect us against any real harm.

On another level, *knowing the Lord* would certainly have meant *knowing the Law* literally, whether the law of Moses or the law of Jesus, but would also mean knowing the law more than literally, so that we can act out of the law from a deep, instinctive level. And that still has meaning for us today, as we seek to follow the spirit and teaching of Jesus. Then and now, I believe, it would have meant knowing the appropriate ritual as well as the whole history of the people of God. We Quakers don't like that word *ritual,* but, in fact, anthropologists can see much ritual in Quakerism, and we are far safer if we have really studied it so that we may both make best use of it and also be free of it at the same time.

Finally, *knowing the Lord* is a matter of the heart and the will and the mind and the spirit, without which, as George Fox implied, religion is but an intellectual or artistic game. *Knowing the Lord* is knowing Him through the first four focus commandments, especially as we follow the expansion of the first commandment in Deuteronomy 6:4,5 and in the words of Jesus. *Knowing the Lord* means giving the entire attention, the whole focus, to the Divine Center, just as Whittier's "Quaker of the Olden Time" did, and just as most of the Quaker ministers of the old style sought to do, even for the making of little daily decisions.[1]

When we say we *know* our child or parent or spouse or friend, or even a beloved employer, we come to know instinctively what that person will like or not like; we don't need to ask! Also, when we really *know* such a person, we don't even have to talk to feel our communion; we can enjoy just being together. So it is in *knowing* God. Hosea, or God speaking through him, recognized the importance of *knowing* God from the heart when he said, "They do not cry to me from the heart, but they wail upon their beds" (Hosea 7:14).

Another key word from Hosea is *Hesed,* which is sometimes translated as mercy or faithfulness or love or steadfastness, but which I like to call *faithful covenant love.* Through the story and images of the first three chapters, Hosea shows us how *faithful covenant love* can be shown by God to an errant people or by one spouse to another. Hosea gives us a model for the faithful and enduring spouse, for the faithful and enduring parent, for the faithful and enduring friend, and for the faithful and enduring helper. These chapters also give us a model for returning that *faithful covenant love* to God. Although we can find some mention of Divine love earlier in the Scriptures, it is Hosea who expanded the prophetic awareness of God's love, an awareness which continued to grow in power until it flowered with the coming of Jesus. This new understanding of love which comes down to us from Hosea means more than our single word *love* usually implies for love can be both shallow and selfish. Therefore, it is important to call it *covenant love,* for this implies a profound and irrevocable agreement to care for and to sustain the other. Thus, it is not merely affectionate love which holds an ideal marriage together, it is *covenant love,* a love which stands by the other, no matter what. Hosea reminds that parenting is also an act of covenant, requiring the same kind of absolute, unshakable support for the child; just as growing up in that security helps the grown-up child return that love to the aging parent. However, the word *covenant* can be limiting if it implies a legalistic caring, so it is good to add the word *faithful,* giving us *faithful covenant love,* the kind of love God has for us, and without which, says God through Hosea, our families, our nation, and our meetings will become disorganized.

Finally, Hosea speaks to us across the centuries when he distills his message from God into one sentence containing two of the key words: ''For I desire steadfast love and not sacrifice, the knowledge of God rather than burnt offerings'' (Hosea 6:6).

Several decades later, after the powerful northern kingdom

had indeed been destroyed as Amos and Hosea had foreseen, another small-town prophet, Micah, took up God's demand for human justice, this time in the southern kingdom of Judah. Although Micah did not have the wealth, the education, the political connections, or even the literary style of his contemporary, the great prophet Isaiah of Jerusalem, he left behind him a passionate, almost angry plea for justice. He also left us, like Amos and Hosea, a wonderful summary of the prophetic message, one upon which we can still meditate fruitfully today:

> "With what shall I come before the Lord, and bow myself
> before God on high? Shall I come before him with burnt
> offerings, with calves a year old; Will the Lord be pleased with
> thousands of rams, with ten thousands of rivers of oil: shall
> I give my first-born for my transgression, the fruit of my
> body for the sin of my soul?" He has showed you, O people,
> what is good; and what does the Lord require of you, but to do
> justice, to love kindness, and to walk humbly with your God?
> (Micah 6:6-8)

We can translate the first part of this familiar statement into our own time and culture by saying something like this: "How can I justify myself before almighty God; how can I justify my existence in a world where so many are miserable; what offering from me can possibly please God; what is the right sharing of my resources in this wealthy and privileged land; what percentage of my talents and time must I give to God, or on behalf of God, to feel inward peace? What great sacrifice must I make, such as giving up TV or my car or my insurance policy or my career in order to justify myself and feel peace within?" The quiet, confident, and very simple answer comes back across 2700 years: The way to please God, and to find inward peace, lies not in the numbers game of deciding just how much of my treasure will please God, for that is the way of "works righteousness." The rough but very practical prophet Micah saw that the way to please God is not in a giving or sacrificing which leaves the heart untouched, but in *doing* and *being:* to *do* justice (not just to believe in it), to *love* mercy (faithful covenant love), and *to walk humbly with God.*

I am glad that Micah added the last expression, ''to walk humbly with God,'' for that brings a dynamic, evolving unity and power to the other key words of the prophets. The Old Testament use of this phrase has many rich meanings which could include our Quaker attempt to follow the moment-by-moment and day-by-day leadings of the Holy Spirit, so that we depend not merely on a traditional knowledge of the recorded law, but we can be open to continuing revelation as we face the circumstances of each new day. ''To walk with God'' could also mean a life of real purity and focus, as was true of Enoch, who ''walked with God'' (Genesis 5:22). Finally, to ''walk with God'' implies knowing and being in contact with God, like a prophet of old. I confess I find it a bit scary when I contemplate these queries and advices of the prophet Micah, for I realize that I can no longer say whether I am to give one percent or ten percent of my self and substance, for I feel that I shall be asked to give all of myself to that living focus with the divine.

These four key ideas from the prophets—*justice, knowledge of God, faithful covenant love,* and *walking with God*—bring us back to the paradox of the Quaker understanding of Christianity; we are called to both a powerful inwardness and to a powerful outwardness at the same time. The prophets demand active, measurable, ethical behavior from us *outwardly,* but they also insist on a special quality of being, *inwardly.* Howard Brinton spanned this paradox by describing Quakerism as an ethical mysticism. Sometimes I attempt to explain this paradox by describing Quakerism as a nonverbal form of Christianity; that is, we follow Christ in placing much emphasis on *outward* behavior and service, we follow Christ in placing much emphasis on the reality of *inward experience* which makes the outward behavior possible, but we put less emphasis on verbal theological statements *about* Christ.

The danger of isolating these key words from the prophets is that they may become just that—just words handed down from one generation to the next. One key to converting these "mere words" into personal reality lies in the experience of personal transformation (however we define it theologically) as described by several hundred Quaker journalists over three centuries. For some Quaker prophets the transformation has been as quick and sudden as it appeared to have been for the prophet Isaiah, who wrote:

> In the year that King Uzziah died I saw the Lord sitting upon a throne, high and lifted up; and his train filled the temple. Above him stood the seraphim; each had six wings: with two he covered his face, and with two he covered his feet, and with two he flew. And one called to another and said: "Holy, holy, holy is the Lord of hosts; the whole earth is full of his glory." And the foundations of the thresholds shook at the voice of him who called, and the house was filled with smoke. And I said: "Woe is me! For I am lost; for I am a man of unclean lips, and I dwell in the midst of a people of unclean lips; for my eyes have seen the King, the Lord of Hosts!" Then flew one of the seraphim to me, having in his hand a burning coal which he had taken with tongs from the altar. And he touched my mouth, and said: "Behold, this has touched your lips; your guilt is taken away, and your sin forgiven." And I heard the voice of the Lord saying, "Whom shall I send, and who will go for us?" Then I said, "Here am I! Send me." (Isaiah 6:1-8)

This type of experience still happens in our own time, though not, of course, in exactly the same language or in exactly the same way. There still comes, to certain individuals, the same shaking awareness of the awesome power at the center of the universe before whom our great civilizations are but matchsticks in the cosmic wind. Yet in the same instant they are told that this Power cares about us and yearns to guide our evolution into the New Age.

Most of us will not be called to the prominence of the work of an Isaiah, but we are called to be prophets, each according to the grace given to us. Although the Bible records only the one dramatic incident about Isaiah's call and purification, he was probably as well prepared—or even more thoroughly prepared—than were Samuel and Saul for that moment when God's power burst in upon them. What then is our preparation today for entering that same and living stream? Do we, like the Biblical prophets and their more recent successors, devote ourselves to a daily spiritual discipline appropriate to our stage of the spiritual journey? Do we cultivate a personal or group worship which can open us to the prophetic stream?

The Stubborn Joy, The Cross Of Joy

When we pass through the dark times of our own lives or the discouraging moments of history, it is good to know the prophet Habakkuk, for he asked the questions we all ask. He not only asked the question, but he—or God through him—gave an answer which can lead to the amazing power of the cross of joy. We know very little about this man except that he probably lived and prophesied about a hundred years after the work of Micah and his contemporary, Isaiah. During the time of Isaiah there had been one miraculous delivery of Jerusalem from the Assyrians in 701 B.C. (Isaiah 38), but in the following century there had been many years when Judah's kings Mannassah and Ammon were politically and religiously under Assyrian domination. Then the boy Josiah became king in 640, just about the time that Assyria began to grow weaker. Josiah was especially faithful to the Old Covenant of Moses, and he made many reforms, especially after someone found what purported to be a very old manuscript of the laws of Moses which scholars think is the core of the book of Deuteronomy. But this good and popular and reforming king was killed in battle by an odd quirk of history in 609 at the time the Assyrian empire was being destroyed for ever. He was followed in quick succession by four kings, two of whom ruled for less than a year. In 597 Judah was captured by the rising empire of Babylon, which would totally destroy Jerusalem and the Jewish state ten years later. It is thought that Habakkuk's anguished prophecy must have occurred after the death of the good king Josiah but before the kingdom of Judah had been annihilated in 587.

All of the great prophets before Habakkuk and his contemporary, Jeremiah, had literally been God's mouthpieces, speaking the words which came through them, just as we know the Quaker ministers of the quietist and Wilburite eras did, but in this anguished time both Jeremiah and Habakkuk started talking back to God, passionately questioning Divine justice, just as some of us ask questions when great souls are assassinated or when the innocent are massacred under tyrants:

> O Lord, how long shall I cry for help, and thou wilt not hear? Or cry to thee, ''Violence!'' and thou wilt not save? Why dost thou make me see wrongs and look upon trouble? Destruction and violence are before me; strife and contention arise. So the law is slacked and justice never goes forth. For the wicked surround the righteous, so justice goes forth perverted. (Habakkuk 1:2-4)

God's answer is not very consoling, for he says:

> Look among the nations, and see; wonder and be astounded. . . . For lo, I am rousing the Chaldeans, that bitter and hasty nation, who march through the breadth of the earth, to seize habitations not their own. (Habakkuk 1:5,6)

The next three verses vividly describe the Chaldeans' ruthless military power, concluding with, "Then they sweep by like the wind and go on, guilty men, whose own might is their god!" (Habakkuk 1:11)

Habakkuk can't take that for an answer, so he tries again with a question which runs from the twelfth to seventeenth verses with these words as the core of his complaint: "Why dost thou look on faithless men, and art silent when the wicked swallows up the man more righteous than he?" Habakkuk ends this section with, "Is he then to keep on emptying his net, and mercilessly slaying nations for ever?"

Finally, in the second chapter, the stubborn prophet climbs his famous watchtower to challenge God:

> I will take my stand to watch, and station myself on the tower, and look forth to see what he will say to me, and what I will answer concerning my complaint. (Habakkuk 2:1)

It is possible that Habakkuk did climb one of the towers in or near Jerusalem, so that he might stare out into the lonely, star-spangled sky, night after night, trying to reconcile his prophetic foreboding with his belief in the faithfulness of God. To use a modern term, he was engaging in one of the spiritual disciplines, such as most prophets of all ages have discovered they must do. We all know that the answer to a spiritual question seldom comes instantly (although it does sometimes) so that the prophets of old and our thirty decades of Quaker prophets often had to stand for hours in what seemed like the darkness of God before the answer came. But the answer does come, in a way which is like what happens after we have entered what seems to be a very dark room. If we just sit and wait patiently in such a room, gradually our eyes adjust to the light which has always been there, and we begin to see patterns and shapes and outlines, whereas before we had seen nothing but darkness. Long and faithful practice of the spiritual disciplines and fervent, focused entrance into the spirit of the gathered meeting do open the way to such seeing and hearing of the vast purposes of God for our little lives.

And so the prophet Habakkuk was at last able to say:

> And the Lord answered me: "Write the vision; make it plain upon tablets, so he may run who reads it. For still the vision awaits its time; it hastens to the end—it will not lie [delay]." (Habakkuk 2:2,3)

In a way this first part of God's response was still not very encouraging: times may be tough now and they must get worse before they can be better! On the other hand, it is always reassuring when a skilled doctor or psychologist or social scientist can look beyond the terrifying surface disorder because they can see it as a stage in the process and can see beyond it to the emerging patterns of a new level of existence. Thus prophets who know the law upon which all creation turns and who continually re-enter the stream of the Living Presence are able to avoid panic in the hurly-burly of the present because of instinctive knowledge of the inevitability of the working out of the Divine law. Such calm does not mean that our prophets will be twiddling their thumbs in a mystical way; they may be very busy—though not frantic.

But God's answer goes on to a statement which has nourished and puzzled the Jewish and Christian reader ever since: "Behold, he whose soul is not upright in him shall fail, but the righteous shall live by his faith" (Habakkuk 2:4). An alternate translation which helps expand this important concept reads, "but the *just* shall live by *faith*" or "the *just* shall live by(or in)*faithfulness. "* As we had learned from Amos, *doing* justice and *being* righteous are inseparable from each other; both the *doing* and the *being* are necessary, even in difficult times. The answer to Habakkuk's question tells us that we can sustain this, year after year, only by faith, by active faithfulness.

For the Apostle Paul this idea became a central part of his vision of the work of Christ:

> For I am not ashamed of the gospel: it is the power of God for salvation to everyone who has faith, to the Jew first and also to the Greek. For in it the righteousness of God is revealed through faith for faith; as it is written, "He who through faith is righteous shall live." (Romans 1:16,17)

Later he wrote:

> But now the righteousness of God has been manifested apart from the law, although the law and prophets bear witness to it, the righteousness of God through faith in Jesus Christ for all who believe. (Romans 3:21,22)

On another occasion he said: "Now it is evident that no man is justified before God by the law; for 'He who through faith is righteous shall live' " (Galatians 3:11).

It is just at this point, in a typical Quaker audience, that some of my readers will begin to turn off, while others will begin to nod approvingly, especially if I were to add some other New Testament passages about the power of faith and about the importance of believing in Christ. I ask those of you who are about to approve of me to withhold that approval for a few moments, and those who are about to disapprove to withhold judgment, for it is precisely in this area, which we might call the geometry and topology of faith, that the Quaker understanding of Christian jargon can be significantly different from that of many other Christians. I use the word *jargon* deliberately but not irreverently here, for the Christian words are important to me.

What then is faith, as the Quakers have understood it? As the term so often comes to us from the writings of Paul and from more recent Christians, *faith* is associated with *belief,* and belief has generally been equated with assent to certain statements, or at least with the ability to say certain words. Even though words are important, the Quaker understanding of faith and of belief is that they are primarily nonverbal. It is almost as if the Friends have traditionally said that the *faith* or the *belief* must come first, and only then can we try to find words to fit them. For example, quite early in his *Journal,* George Fox wrote:

> About the beginning of the year 1646, as I was going to Coventry, and entering towards the gate, a consideration arose in me, how it was said that all Christians are believers, both Protestants and Papists; and the Lord opened to me that, if all were believers, then they were all born of God and passed from death to life, and that none were true believers but such; and that though others said they were believers, yet they were not.[1]

Margaret Fell, who was already an exemplary Christian, was so shaken when she heard George Fox preach in her church that she cried out, "We are all thieves! We are all thieves! We have taken the Scriptures in words and know nothing of them in ourselves."[2] These words of George Fox and Margaret Fell remind us that the powerful faith of Moses and Isaiah came not from the repetition of a creed, but from an ego-shattering experience; the faith-power came before the words. In fact, as we observe the experience of prophets from Moses right up through the coming of the Holy Spirit again and again in the book of Acts, we see that the full faith usually resulted from an experience which transformed the old self, so that the early Christians said, as some do today, that they had been reborn.

One way to comprehend the traditional Quaker experience of faith is to try to find other words for this nonverbal reality. To do that, let's forget the usual religious jargon and use, instead, the word *trust*. This is surely what Jesus meant to convey by describing God as a loving parent. What is it that makes it possible to *trust* your friend or your spouse? Is it not that you *know* that person on some very deep level? This reminds us of Hosea's concern for *knowing God,* which is not just a theological expression; it is a way of saying that because I know God on a real and nonverbal level, because I have communion with that Divine reality, I therefore have a sense of trust so profound that its effects can be measured in my physical body and my emotions.

The Quaker understanding of faith goes even beyond this, for it sees faith as a result of the *inward work of Christ,* which, if we translate the jargon, leads to another nonverbal image for faith which sees it as a quiet flow of energy from the Divine into us, a quiet flow of energy which allows the old and ego-centered self gradually or suddenly to become transformed, making it possible to live more nearly as Christ taught us to live. Thus, the traditional Quaker experience is that faith is largely a result of being in the presence of God. Such faith, like any of our faculties, must be used or it will wither away. Therefore it is often important to use the alternative translation for Habakkuk's answer, *faithfulness,* for a living faith is not merely passive. A living faith, which must involve faithfulness, requires an active responding, a stepping out into the darkness, a trusting that our Divine Friend will support us as we move forward in the dangerous but exciting stream.

Finally, our scientific friends might remind us that there is at least one other way to describe faith. It is no accident that there have been so many Quaker scientists, for scientists are attentive and nonjudgmental observers, as we all should be, if like Habakkuk, we would stand on the watchtower of that quiet, trustful state of consciousness, and wait. The scientist has faith in a conceptual picture of the universe, a universe based upon laws which science is still seeking to understand. Just so, we recognize that each of us already has faith in our own picture or concept of reality. We could do nothing, we would be paralyzed, if we did not have such a nonverbal faith in the reality in which we live and make money and die. If, like Habakkuk, we stand for hours on that watchtower in the presence of God, the shape of reality begins to change, new laws of spiritual cause and effect begin to emerge, and we come to know more and more about the Law which holds the universe together. Thus, over the years, experienced Friends may discover that their faith does include an empowering concept of ultimate reality and its laws. Such Friends might even find it possible to write that down like a creed, but they would never insist that others must believe just those words, for faith comes from observation, experience, and faithfulness.

I was once given a vision of a cross of joy on a New Year's Eve long ago. It came quite by surprise as I sat in my own inward watchtower. Later I learned to describe it as the deep, instinctive awareness of Romans 8:28 where Paul says, ''We know that in everything God works for good with those who love him, who are called according to his purpose.'' At the heart of the Christian experience as exemplified by George Fox and the Quaker tradition, there is a deep and irrepressible joy, even when on the surface of our life we may be embroiled in troubles and confusion. When we go to that quiet inward place, the inward witness tells us that we are to confront these trials with a quiet, relaxed and nonjudgmental joy. And that is where the cross comes in, for there are many times when we don't want to meet these things with joy, and I, at least, would much rather be angry or feel sorry for myself. Yet, if we stay with that cross of joy with the faithfulness of Habakkuk the stubborn prophet, our own spiritual journey will get on much more rapidly, and we shall be more able to hear the voice of God when he calls to be a doing or speaking or praying prophet.

Jeremiah and Ezekiel, two prophets who probably lived during the same anguished time as Habakkuk, also help us to look forward to the new life which would become possible in the New Covenant, and George Fox often loved to quote them to help explain the radical new level of consciousness and the radical changes in life style of the early Friends.

Like other prophets, Jeremiah had a distinct experience of being called by God at a specific time, being told: "Before I formed you in the womb I knew you, and before you were born I consecrated you; I appointed you a prophet to the nations" (Jeremiah 1:5). But, like Moses and many Quakers who were called to become ministers in the earlier Quaker centuries, he resisted, saying: "Ah, Lord God! Behold, I do not know how to speak, for I am only a youth" (Jeremiah 1:6). But the Lord said to him:

> "Do not say 'I am only a youth'; for to all to whom I send you you shall go, and whatever I command you you shall speak. Be not afraid of them, for I am with you to deliver you, says the Lord." (Jeremiah 1:7,8)

In other words, being in the prophetic stream means being open to God and to human suffering while being thick-skinned and strong enough to bear criticism and run great risks. The great prophets, and we who would follow, must be tough and tender at the same time, or as the prophet Jesus said, "wise as serpents and innocent as doves" (Matthew 10:16). The times were so difficult and his prophetic task was so demanding that

Jeremiah was commanded not to marry: ''You shall not take a wife, nor shall you have sons or daughters in this place'' (Jeremiah 16:2). He was forbidden to attend either funerals or wedding feasts. Like Habakkuk, Jeremiah also talked back to God or he wavered bitterly within himself as in this passage describing the anguish of being a prophet:

> If I say, ''I will not mention him, or speak any more in his name,'' there is in my heart as it were a burning fire shut up in my bones, and I am weary with holding it in, and I cannot. (Jeremiah 20:9)

With that kind of prophetic fire burning within him at that point in history, Jeremiah was sure to have a dramatic life, and the book of Jeremiah, which is the longest of the prophetic books, gives more biographical detail than we have on any other prophet. He narrowly escaped death on several occasions, for a time he was imprisoned, and for a time he had to go into hiding; and he was finally carried away from his own land by his own people to Egypt, where, according to tradition, he was martyred. Through all of this he remained faithful to his divine commission, urging people to follow the will of God and not to put their faith in balance-of-power politics and armies; and like all prophets, he urged them to live the law, both the laws of inward focus and the laws of outward justice. His unpopular prophecy began to come true when the bold new empire of Babylon overran Judah, captured Jerusalem, and exiled its leading citizens and nobility to Babylon in 597. While other prophets of that time proclaimed that God would soon bring back the exiles and restore the independence of Judah, Jeremiah had a less popular message. He wrote a letter to the exiles, urging upon them what we might call the cross of joy, telling them to accept their situation, settle down in captivity, and work hard for their own welfare and for the prosperity of the alien land. His letter also contains this promise from

47

the Lord: "When seventy years are completed for Babylon, I will visit you, and I will fulfill to you my promise and bring you back to this place" (Jeremiah 29:10). A few years later, in spite of everything Jeremiah could do, Judah once again failed to heed his warnings and rebelled against Babylon. In 587 Babylonian armies destroyed Jerusalem, exiled many more citizens, and took over the shattered country as a minor province of the new empire.

In addition to offering this fascinating case study of how one prophet lived and worked, the book of Jeremiah has some beautiful passages which look beyond the limitations of the old Law and the Old Covenant which most of the people had not been able to uphold. He prophesied about a new covenant which takes us deeper into the meaning of Habakkuk's "the righteous shall live by his faith." Many Christians, including the early Quakers, believed that this passage pointed toward the New Covenant, the New Testament:

"But this is the covenant which I will make with the house of Israel after those days, says the Lord; I will put my law within them, and I will write in their hearts; and I will be their God, and they shall be my people. And no longer shall each man teach his neighbor and each his brother, saying, 'Know the Lord,' for they shall all know me, from the least of them to the greatest says the Lord; for I will forgive their iniquity, and I will remember their sin no more." (Jeremiah 31:33,34)

Jeremiah's contemporary, the high-ranking priest Ezekiel, was exiled when Jerusalem was captured for the first time, in 597. Like Jeremiah, Ezekiel believed that Jerusalem was doomed and that God would perform no miracle to save the corrupt kingdom; but unlike Jeremiah, Ezekiel had to perform all of his prophecy as an exile in Babylonia. His prophecy also speaks of a new covenant in a way which helps fill in Habakkuk's vision and which helps explain the Quaker experience of faith:

> I will sprinkle clean water on you, and you shall be clean from all your uncleanlinesses, and from all your idols I will cleanse you. A new heart I will give you, and a new spirit I will put within you; and I will take out of your flesh the heart of stone and give you a heart of flesh. And I will put my spirit within you, and cause you to walk in my statutes and be careful to observe my ordinances. (Ezekiel 36:25-27)

George Fox and early Friends found Jeremiah's and Ezekiel's words a good description of their own experience. For example, Ezekiel's version of the New Covenant speaks of cleansing; however we describe it theologically or psychologically, the early Friends did experience a freedom from sin and the proclivity to sin, as if the true focus of the focus commandments had been restored. Ezekiel speaks of being given a new heart as different as living flesh is from cold stone; in the power of the spirit, many, many Quakers have discovered a capacity for tenderness and steadfastness they had not known before. Jeremiah's version has God saying, "I will put my law within them, and I will write it in their hearts." Generations of Quaker prophets have had the awesome experience of discovering that the law is indeed written in the heart of one who has climbed Habakkuk's watchtower of silent waiting before the Lord, again and again. Jeremiah's version says that in the New Covenant: "No longer shall each man teach his neighbor and each his brother, saying, 'know the Lord,' for they shall all know me, from the least of them to the greatest" (Jeremiah 31:34). It is no accident that the Society of Friends has traditionally had a radically different pattern of church leadership, a radically different pattern of ministry, and even a different concept of education, because of early Friends' living experience of the reality of God's presence in all who had truly opened to the Spirit, just as Jeremiah had predicted. Finally, the clincher, the *empowering* aspect of the New Covenant, an important dynamic of the Quaker experience of faith, comes from Ezekiel's version: "And I will put my spirit within you, and cause you to walk in my statutes, and be careful to observe my ordinances" (Ezekiel 36:27). Thus, faith means more than trust; in some mysterious way it also means empowerment. It means the ability to walk with God even in dark and difficult places as we follow the otherwise impossible law of the prophet Jesus, remembering Habakkuk's answer: "The righteous shall *live* by . . . . faith [and faithfulness]" (Habakkuk 2:4).

TAKING JESUS DOWN FROM THE WALL

> I will raise up for them a prophet like you [Moses] from among their brethren; and I will put my words in his mouth, and he shall speak to them all that I command him. (Deuteronomy 18:18)

Both the early Christians and George Fox believed that Jesus was the prophet like Moses who was to come after Moses. The trouble was that Jesus, the living, present prophet, was not available to George Fox when he began to seek. Jesus Christ had been stuck up on the wall in an impressive and magnificent way, but he was completely out of reach to the ordinary person. The teen-age George Fox believed the gospel story of Jesus' life, death, and resurrection, and he believed Jesus was his savior in a legal way, but that made no difference to his actual daily life. Jesus was stuck on the wall of the church, quite honorably, and he was stuck back across 1600 years of history, or he was stuck far off into the future when he would be the final judge.

For some of the same as well as different reasons, Jesus, the present and living prophet, has not been available to multitudes in our own time. One cause may be that the modern mind has been out of touch with our intuitive ability to feel nonverbal religious reality. Biblical scholarship, in spite of its tremendous value, has for some people undermined the reality of the Old or New Testament stories. What we popularly call science has, for several generations, influenced many people to disbelieve in Jesus because they could not believe in miracles. Other sensitive people have been turned away from Jesus because they perceived a rigidity in the only Christianity they knew, a rigidity which permitted or upheld segregation and oppression and which too easily went to war in the name of Christ, a rigidity which too easily saw evil as incarnated in communists, other races, or homosexuals, or liberals, or conservatives, without recognizing that the roots of evil must always first be faced within ourselves. And some, who have not had a chance to read Quaker history from the inside and have not met the "feminist" side of George and Margaret Fell Fox, have been turned away from an available Christ because of the word *he,* because of Paul's views about women, and because of the inferior status of women throughout most of Christianity. And some of my friends are wary of Christ because of the strong religious exclusiveness they find in many vocal Christians.

I believe that Christ is available in our time because George Fox and others have rediscovered a living Christ different from the conventional image on the wall. To understand the Quaker interpretation of Christianity we need to go back to the Suffering Servant passages in a part of the book of Isaiah which was probably written during the exile. The prophets' predictions about the destruction of Judah had finally come true in 587, at which time a second large band of leading citizens was exiled to Babylon. Among these captives and the group which had been sent ten years earlier there must have been members of an informal association which had cherished the teachings of Isaiah for over a century. Thanks to these disciples and to the strenuous work of the exile prophet Ezekiel, the exiles did not lose their religion when they left the turf of their old God. They remembered Jeremiah's letter to them, and they became even more fervent in their devotion to a God who now had no temple, but whom they discovered could be worshiped anywhere. And so they prospered and worshiped and waited in an alien land.

About the middle of that century, while there were many exiles who could still remember Jerusalem, the international and political scene began to change. A new world power was rapidly rising in Persia, and the renewed Babylonian empire, so dominant and invincible under Nebuchadnezzar, was growing rotten at the core. Many of the exiles had grown prosperous during their half-century in the cosmopolitan environment of the land of Babylon, but they had not forgotten their God who still refused to be imprisoned in a word, a creed or an icon. They treasured, read and re-read the old sacred writings and the more recent scrolls of the prophets who proved to have been so very right. One of those inspired readers, who was very familiar with the work of Isaiah, or perhaps even part of a fellowship descended from his disciples, began to feel that terrible and exciting call to speak as a prophet. Thus, what we know as the fortieth through the fifty-fifth chapters of Isaiah were spoken bit by bit or prophetic burst by prophetic burst 150 years after the original Isaiah, by someone steeped in Isaiah's language and thought. Beyond that, the writer of these inspiring passages remains completely anonymous. Quite early his work was added to the scroll of the original Isaiah, with all hint of separate authorship lost until modern scholarship recognized what we now often call *Second Isaiah.*

Second Isaiah, whoever he was, received what George Fox would have called great openings about the arising stream of spiritual power which was about to re-enter the remnant of his people. How different he sounds from the earlier prophets as he begins:

> Comfort, comfort my people, says your God. Speak tenderly to Jerusalem, and cry to her that her warfare is ended, that her iniquity is pardoned, that she has received from the Lord's hand double for all her sins. (Isaiah 40:1-2)

The God who speaks through Second Isaiah seems a far vaster God than we have met before in the Old Testament; he is the God of the entire planet and all its peoples and all of history. Yet the tenderness, the nurturing and sustaining power of God is also a very strong theme for Second Isaiah, who uses terms like *redeemer,* which will be expanded in later Christian centuries. This mighty God, to whom "the nations are like a drop from a bucket, and are accounted as the dust on the scales" (Isaiah 40:15) is the God who invites all people to that watchtower of worship, of altered consciousness:

> "Ho, everyone who thirsts, come to the waters; and he who has no money, come, buy and eat! Come, buy wine and milk without money and without price." (Isaiah 55:1)

And he promises:

> They who wait for the Lord shall renew their strength, they shall mount up with wings like eagles, they shall run and not be weary, they shall walk and not faint. (Isaiah 40:31)

Second Isaiah's Suffering Servant songs have intrigued both scholars and devout readers for many centuries. To be honest, I must say that these songs, like all great literature, are open to several beautiful and different interpretations which have inspired Jew and Christian alike. They also inspired the young Jesus, who early in his ministry read a Servant song from Isaiah in his hometown synagogue.[1] One way of getting closer to the spirit of Jesus is to look at these songs which apparently influenced him in a profound way. Through them we can enter into the mind and heart of the historic and eternal Christ, getting behind all that verbal theology which had frozen him into a static image on the wall for many people.

The first and shortest of these songs about the coming servant of the Lord mentions *justice* three times in four verses:

> Behold my servant, whom I uphold, my chosen, in whom my soul delights; I have put my Spirit upon him, he will bring forth justice to the nations. He will not cry or lift up his voice, or make it heard in the street; a bruised reed he will not break, and a dimly burning wick he will not quench; he will faithfully bring forth justice. He will not fail or be discouraged till he has established justice in the earth; and the coastlands wait for his law. (Isaiah 42:1-4)

In the first verse we notice how justice and spirit go together, just as justice and righteousness before God were inseparable for the earlier prophets: ''I have put my spirit upon him [and as a result] he will bring forth justice to the nations.'' This justice is to be given not only to the Jews or the future Christians, but ''to the nations.''

Everything in the second and third verses seems to be related to *justice,* which is their concluding word. These verses lead me to ponder the powerful gentleness of the historic Jesus and to appreciate the quiet way of the Holy Spirit as it brings us to our knees before the law of justice. True justice, the justice we all seek, is more akin to healing than to punishment, to a renewed and higher harmony than to rigid organization. Thus, far back in the Old Testament we find seeds of the insight so precious to Friends that the means do determine the ends, for this Servant-to-come will use gentle means, for only so can he bring the justice which is true healing, true health, true order.

The last verse tells us that the Suffering Servant is like a wedge which is slowly, imperceptibly opening the heart of humanity so that true justice may grow. The power of that advancing wedge of Christ is infinite and absolute, even if very slow and gentle; it will never be discouraged because its root and source is faithful covenant love. And let us note the powerful universalism as we re-read the last verse: "He will not fail or be discouraged till he has established justice in the earth; and the coastlands wait for his law."

In another Servant song the Servant himself speaks:

> The Lord God has given me the tongue of those who are taught, that I may know how to sustain with a word him that is weary. Morning by morning he wakens, he wakens my ear to hear as those who are taught. (Isaiah 50:4)

Remembering that this passage may have influenced Jesus' picture of himself, we can also remember Jesus' spiritual disciplines—the long times of prayer and solitude in which he allowed himself to be taught so that he might have the tongue of the taught, an incredibly gentle but powerful gift with words. This passage also suggests the marvelous economy of Jesus' words. Just as we were told in the last song that the Servant would not need to shout and make a big noise, we see that it takes only a few well-chosen words to encourage, just as the most powerful medicine often comes in the smallest dose to heal. The theme of the Servant as faithful listener goes on in the next two verses as we again think of the spiritual disciplines of the Servant:

> The Lord God has opened my ear, and I was not rebellious, I turned not backward. I gave my back to the smiters, and my cheeks to those who pulled out the beard; I hid not my face from shame and spitting. (Isaiah 50:5,6)

55

Because he has been so deeply taught, because he has listened so obediently, the Servant is able to live out that law of gentleness, that awareness that the means do beget the ends. However, his steadfastness comes not only from obedient listening; it also comes from the active experience of faith:

> For the Lord God helps me; therefore I have not been confounded; Therefore I have set my face like a flint, and I know I shall not be put to shame; he who vindicates me is near. (Isaiah 50:7)

Time after time these verses have helped me take down the distant picture of Jesus Christ and brought me closer not only to the historic Jesus of Galilee, but also to the cosmic and gentle presence which I have felt in my own heart. As we seek to pattern our own lives after Jesus' example, this song suggests how we can can allow the Holy Spirit to awaken us morning by morning to hear as those who are taught. It is wonderful to find that clear inward awareness, not only as we waken into each new day, but even during the night, or at any moment of the day. And sometimes that clear inward presence gives us a word, a touch, or even a silent thought which can sustain another. Many times, of course, it is we who are sustained by the Word of that presence within us. Many Quaker journals and many living Friends witness to the living and effective nonviolence which comes out of the discipline of such listening, a nonviolence which grows out of faith as Quakers understand it; that is, faith as inward experience and inward empowerment.

The Servant song which probably meant the most to the early Christians begins:

> Behold, my servant shall prosper, he shall be exalted and lifted up, and shall be very high. As many were astonished at him—his appearance was so marred, beyond human semblance, and his form beyond that of the sons of men—so shall he startle many nations; kings shall shut their

mouths because of him; for that which has not been told them they shall see, and that which they have not heard they shall understand. (Isaiah 52:13-15)

Part of the text is difficult here, perhaps because a copyist of long ago made a mistake, but something of Jesus' profound and unconventional humility as well as his suffering and sacrifice seemed to speak to the earliest Christians and to those who followed them. The song goes on in the next chapter:

Who has believed what we have heard? And to whom has the arm of the Lord been revealed? For he grew up before him like a young plant, and like a root out of dry ground; he had no form or comeliness that we should look at him, and no beauty that we should desire him. (Isaiah 53:1,2)

As we move into the third verse, we can see why, even though there are good arguments for this not being an exact prophecy of Jesus, many have seen these verses as pointing to him. And as we read this entire song, it is good to remember that Jesus read it and was apparently profoundly influenced by it:

He was despised and rejected by men; a man of sorrows, and acquainted with grief; and as one from whom men hide their faces he was despised, and we esteemed him not. Surely he has borne our griefs and carried our sorrows; yet we esteemed him stricken, smitten by God, and afflicted. But he was wounded for our transgressions, he was bruised for our iniquities; upon him was the chastisement that made us whole, and with his stripes are we healed. (Isaiah 53:3-5)

It was at this point that I, in my youthful objection to the words and creeds and psychological pressure of some vocal Christians, had to argue. I was offended to think that my salvation depended upon substitutionary magic and such physical violence.

However, reading the prophets, including these parts of Second Isaiah, and standing for many hours on that watchtower of a consciousness opened toward God, have revealed a deeper meaning—beyond the violent physical imagery—of the Christ event in history. For me, an important way to understand or comprehend what Fox called the *outward* work of Christ upon the cross is to understand how Jesus was able to identify with all humanity. Most prophets had this ability to *feel* for their people; thus, they groaned mightily for their people and prayed mightily to God for them. Read the journals of our Quaker prophets and you will find the same painful faculty.[2] Jesus, as the culmination and fulfillment of the Hebrew prophets, had an intense capacity to identify with the entire human race and even, as some would say, with all creation. The fact that he died painfully upon a Roman torture device is but a parochial detail in comparison to his cosmic work of dying to the self on behalf of humanity. Of course, we could spend several pages defining the term "dying to the self," which also used to be offensive to me because it seemed to be life denying instead of life affirming. Later I learned to see it as part of the process of personal transformation into the next stage of human evolution.

When Jesus died 2000 years ago, he began a process which can remove the curse of individualism which is threatening to destroy our planet.

> All we like sheep have gone astray; we have turned everyone to his own way; and the Lord has laid on him the iniquity of us all. He was oppressed, and he was afflicted, yet he opened not his mouth; like a lamb that is led to the slaughter, and like a sheep that before its shearers is dumb, so he opened not his mouth. (Isaiah 53:6,7)

Here and in verses eight and nine of this chapter, we are given one more picture of a powerful and gentle nonviolence which is sustained by a faith in the living law at the core of all life.

The concluding verses of the song mention the substitutionary death of the Suffering Servant in several ways: ". . . . he makes himself an offering for sin," (Isaiah 53:10); ". . . he shall bear their iniquities," (Isaiah 53:11); and " . . . he poured out his soul to death, . . . he bore the sin of many, and made intercession for the transgressors" (Isaiah 53:12). In order to avoid basing my faith on an emotional attachment to a miserable death by public torture, I have been uplifted many times by these words. "By his knowledge shall the righteous one, my servant, make many to be accounted righteous; and he shall bear their iniquities" (Isaiah 53:11). Here we are brought back to that key word in so many of the prophets—the word *knowledge,* which for them and for Jesus really meant *knowing* God. Jesus as Suffering Servant and prophet knew God so totally that his dying to the self performed what seemed like magic, even though it was the working out of law. You may have experienced this knowledge in a small way when in the presence of an individual great soul. When near such a person I have sometimes known things inwardly that I would not ordinarily know, or received inward answers to questions. Such people seem to bring a degree of clarity and peace to those who are in their aura or energy field, especially if we are in tune with them. Thus, it becomes easy for me to believe that Jesus knew God so totally and so obediently that his energy field merged with the Divine Life and encompassed all creation, changing, through his *knowledge* and his self-giving in accordance with that *knowledge,* the psychic climate for all of us, making the Holy Spirit available to all as it had never been before. And so, with this understanding, I read this passage one more time. "By his *knowledge* shall the righteous one, my servant, make many to be accounted righteous, and he shall bear their iniquities."

In one of his first great openings, George Fox heard the words: "There is one, even Christ Jesus, who can speak to thy condition.''[3] Throughout the rest of his long and active life George often used conventional Christian language and endless Bible quotations, but he always used them with a difference because his experience had made Christ a present, living reality rather than a theological statement or an inaccessible, distant diety. I am convinced that Fox can still help take the two-dimensional Jesus down from the wall for us if we become acquainted with his rich and varied ways for describing the inward work of Christ. Fox and early Friends accepted the outward work of Christ, but they insisted that it is this inward work which transforms us and guides us into new ways of ethical behavior, new ways of service, and new ways of fellowship. In other words, George Fox might say that 300 years of Quaker testimonies have arisen from that continuing inward work of Christ, which not only opens us to concerns, but also gives us the power to live them out, to testify, and if need be, to suffer.

George Fox used a wonderful variety of words to describe the wordless; it is as if he has used a many-sided prism to break up the dazzling white light at the center into its many colors or functions, so that we may see it in dynamic rather than static theological ways. Technically, these functions are the ''offices'' of Christ. Lewis Benson, a contemporary George Fox scholar, has alerted our generation of Friends to Fox's way of transforming the static Jesus into a many-splendored rainbow of functions or ''offices'' of Christ working within and through us. According to Benson's research, Fox most frequently mentioned the office of Christ the prophet, that is, the living inward presence which discerns, admonishes, teaches and leads.[4] Fox's next most frequent terms for this inward power were shepherd, bishop, priest, counsellor, and head. As Fox multiplied the ways of describing Christ, he also moved away from the limitations of gender and of male-dominated religious imagery. For example, Fox's second most common term is, as he used it, a term of nurture, of spiritual feeding. Each of the words for Christ denotes a function, a dynamic process rather than a static idea which can be frozen in a flat picture. Gender becomes increasingly irrelevant (just as Jesus said it would be in heaven) as we are called to focus not on the flat word, but on the process which it represents.

And so George Fox invites us out into the midst of the prophetic stream by giving us a variety of words for the inward-working and transforming Christ of his own experience. These terms can become more than words only as we ponder them and step gingerly or boldly into that stream:

teacher. . .
  governor (think of the governor of a steam engine) . . .
    redeemer . . .
      minister (try the older meanings of the word) . . .
        the rock . . . the foundation . . .
          sanctifier . . . your sanctuary . . .
            your way . . . your life . . .
              heavenly seasoner . . .
                orderer (justice, harmony) . . .
                  wisdom of God . . . treasure of wisdom . . .
                    truth . . .
                      the door . . .
                        light power . . . a covenant of light . . .
                        a maker of prophets . . .

NOTES

MOSES AND THE ROCK WHERE JOY BEGINS

1. For key excerpts of Fox's "openings" up to 1652, taken from his *Journal,* see *Early Prophetic Openings of George Fox* (Philadelphia: Tract Association of Friends, 1962); for examples of dramatic prophetic action among early Friends, see William C. Braithwaite, *The Second Period of Quakerism,* 2nd. ed. (York, England: William Sessions Limited, 1979), p. 602 and specific cases p. 25(Solomon Eccles); pp. 339, 340(Barclay and Andrew Jaffray); p. 216(Elizabeth Adams); p. 238(John Browne); see also Kenneth Carroll, "Early Quakers and Going Naked as a Sign," *Quaker History* 67, no. 2(Autumn 1978).

2. Those who are offended by the patriarchal tone of the Old Testament will note that the Old Testament wisdom is most often personified as *she.* For examples, see Proverbs 8 and the Wisdom of Solomon 7:22.

3. Martin Buber, *Moses*(London: East and West Library, 1946), p. 52; Bernard W. Anderson, *Understanding the Old Testament*(Englewood Cliffs, New Jersey: Prentice Hall, 1975), pp. 52-56.

4. When speaking to Quaker audiences, I still call it the *Quaker way to read the Bible* in order to reclaim an old Quaker skill; however, the Benedictines, other monastics, and the early Church Fathers and Mothers knew long ago of this way to read.

5. Anderson, *Understanding the Old Testament,* pp. 85, 86.

6. See John L. Nickalls, ed., *The Journal of George Fox* (Cambridge: University Press, 1952), p. 27 where Fox says, "Now I was come up in spirit through the flaming sword into the paradise of God. All things were new, and all the creation gave another smell unto me than before, beyond what words can utter. I knew nothing but pureness, and innocency, and righteousness, being renewed up into the image of God by Christ Jesus, so that I say I was come up to the state of Adam which he was in before he fell." Fox's use of "the flaming sword" is a reference to the expulsion of Adam and Eve from the Garden of Eden: "He drove them out; and at the east of the Garden of Eden he placed the cherubim, and a flaming sword which turned every way to guard the way to the tree of life" (Genesis 3:24).

7. Nickalls, ed., *The Journal of George Fox,* p. 23.

8. George Fox, "Gospel Truth Demonstrated," Vol. 2 in *A Collection of Doctrinal Books,* Vol. 5 of 8, 2nd. ed. (Philadelphia and New York: Marcus T. C. Gould and Isaac T. Hopper, 1831), p. 152. In a supplement to "A Testimony of What we Believe of Christ" (pp. 84-154), George Fox cites I Corinthians 10:4 and then asks, "So is not Christ called a spiritual rock, and was not this before he was born of the Virgin?"

IS CATCHING PROPHECY LIKE CATCHING MEASLES?

1. Like Moses in Exodus or the charismatic leaders in the book of Judges, Saul was regarded as being another person, with greatly enhanced leadership abilities after the Spirit had manifested within him. However, King Saul lost this charisma, or gift of the Spirit, during his reign after being disobedient to the Spirit.

2. For examples of ecstatic worship, see the stories about Elijah and Elisha from I Kings 17 through II Kings 8; B. Anderson discusses Isaiah's disciples in *Understanding the Old Testament,* pp. 314, 315.

3. George Fox, "The Epistles," Vol. 1, Epistle 240 in *A Collection of Doctrinal Books,* Vol. 7 of 8, p. 267.

4. Persons interested in exploring Quaker journals should begin with Howard Brinton, *Quaker Journals* (Wallingford, Pennsylvania: Pendle Hill Publications, 1972). He quotes excerpts from many journals and lists over a hundred in the bibliography.

5. Benjamin Seebohm, comp., *Memoirs of the Life and Gospel Labors of Stephen Grellet,* Vol. 1(Philadelphia: Henry Longstreth, 1860), pp. 20-25; Caroline Stephen, *Quaker Strongholds*(London, 1890), pp. 4,5.

6. Dean Frieday, ed., *Barclay's Apology in Modern English* (Philadelphia, 1967), p. 253.

OPENING SOME KEY WORDS FROM THE PROPHETS

1. Such moment by moment dependence on the "Inward Guide" has never been limited to Quakers! However, the expectation of such attentiveness to the "inward motion" was originally a very important component of Quaker "doctrine" and life style. This can be borne out by reading, almost at random, Quaker journals up through the 19th century, and even some published in this century.

THE STUBBORN JOY, THE CROSS OF JOY

1. Nickalls, ed., *The Journal of George Fox,* p. 7.

2. *Christian Faith and Practice in the Experience of the Society of Friends* (London Yearly Meeting, 1960 printing), extract 20.

TAKING JESUS DOWN FROM THE WALL

1. See Luke 4:16-19 where Jesus reads Isaiah 61:1,2. Many scholars believe that this section of Isaiah was written after the time of Second Isaiah; they call chapters 56 to 66 *Third Isaiah.*

2. John Woolman (1720-1772) is the best known example of a Quaker minister who felt the burden of others, especially in regard to slavery. A lesser known and somewhat more provincial example is Ann Branson (1808-1891).

3. Nickalls, ed. *The Journal of George Fox,* p. 11.

4. Lewis Benson, *What Did George Fox Teach about Christ?* (New Foundations Publications, 1976), p. 4.

PENDLE HILL is a residential study center and a retreat and conference center as well as being the publisher of Pendle Hill books and pamphlets. It is a center for the nurture of religious life and an adult school for intensive study in those fields which help unfold the meaning of life. At Pendle Hill education is thought of in its broadest sense—the transforming of persons and of society.

Pendle Hill offers a three-term **residential program** from October to June. 35 to 40 persons, ranging in age from 19 to 75, enroll as students for one or more terms, joining the resident staff and families. About half the community are Friends. Among the rest a wide variety of faiths, philosophies, and cultural backgrounds is represented. Students pursue interests and concerns through study, reading, writing, meditation, dialogue, and creative projects. Each morning residents gather in **meeting for worship,** held after the manner of Friends. Pendle Hill offers five or six **courses** in the areas of Quakerism, Bible, religious thought, peace and social concerns, literature and the arts, and crafts. Every student participates in the **work program,** helping with the upkeep of house and grounds and with food preparation and meal clean-up.

Admission to Pendle Hill is based upon the applicant's commitment to learning, openness to exploring religious reality, and readiness to take a responsible part in the common life of Pendle Hill. Limited **financial aid** is available for applicants unable to pay the full fees.

Pendle Hill also offers a full program of short term events through its **Extension Program:** weekend conferences and retreats; summer workshops, conferences, and retreats; a series of Monday Evening Lectures; weekly extension courses for persons not living at Pendle Hill. Persons wishing a short term experience in the resident community may also apply to be **sojourners** during most of the year.

Further details on dates and fees for all programs are available from **Pendle Hill, Wallingford, PA 19086. 215-566-4507.**